D1522512

At the Rainbow

AT THE RAINBOW

Poems by Robert Vasquez

MARY BURRITT POETRY SERIES

University of New Mexico Press

Albuquerque

Library of Congress Cataloging-
in-Publication Data
At the rainbow: poems /
by Robert Vasquez.
p. cm. — (Mary Burritt
poetry series)
ISBN 0-8263-1629-8 (CL)
ISBN 0-8263-1630-1 (PA)
1. Mexican Americans—
California—Poetry.
I. Title.
II. Series.
PS3572.A855A8   1995
811'.54—DC20   94-48733
                               CIP

" Bobbin Boy in a Mill in Chicopee,
Mass., 1911, a Photograph by Lewis W.
Hine," "Brothers," "Letter from a New
Widow to Her Son/*after Williams*,"
"Sanitarium, Guadalajara," and "Willing
Witnesses" originally appeared in *Sage*;
all (except for "Sanitarium, Guadalajara")
were reprinted in the anthology *Piecework:
19 Fresno Poets* (Albany, Calif.: Silver
Skates).

"At the Rainbow," "Dia de los Muertos,"
and "Pismo, 1959" originally appeared in
The New England Review; "Dia de los
Muertos" also appeared in the anthology
After Aztlan: Latino Poets of the Nineties
(Boston: David R. Godine).

"Night-song in Verano" originally
appeared in *The Missouri Review*.

"Coyotes" originally appeared in *Plough-
shares*. It was reprinted in *After Aztlan*.

"Early Morning Test Light Over Nevada,
1955" originally appeared in the anthology
New Voices, 1979-1983 (New York: Academy of American Poets). It was reprinted
in *Piecework* and *After Aztlan*.

An earlier version of this manuscript
received the James D. Phelan Literary
Award from the San Francisco
Foundation.

Acknowledgments

My thanks to Joe Barba, Simone Di Piero, Peter Everwine, Ken Fields, Ray Gonzalez, Garrett Hongo, Terry Hummer, Connie Lake, Dixie Lane, Herbert Leibowitz, Phil Levine, Jack Miles, Chuck Moulton, Michael Ryan, Greg Seastrom, Ernesto Trejo, Jon Veinberg, Derek Walcott, Chuck Wasserburg, and many others who've encouraged or influenced my work.

Special thanks to DeWayne Rail, the poet/teacher who helped a full-time worker in his early twenties discover poetry.

And, most of all, I want to thank Ken Butler and Jean Janzen for the priceless gift of their friendship and their poetry.

I greatly appreciate the financial support from the Academy of American Poets, the National Society of Arts & Letters, the National Writers Union, the San Francisco Foundation, and "the farm" for my two years on the peninsula.

Finally, I'll be forever grateful to Lucille Clifton and Beth Jarock of the AWP: total strangers who cared enough to help make this book possible.

for Jose Mercado Vasquez
and Frances Roman Vasquez

. . . I like the idea that nothing
in decades has changed: the garage
still a bedroom; grapes
my father hung on nails
still drying in the toolshed;
the ceramic pink flamingoes
atop the TV, the matching
birds in the mirror about to drink
from the eyes of my mother,
who stares when alone, whose stare
I've inherited and carry
into years of rooms where I
will be alone; the dirt corner
beyond the bedroom window where
I can take aim at cactus and,
with BBs through green
flesh, leave my mark.

Contents

I.

Coyotes 3
Belief 6
Early Morning Test Light Over Nevada, 1955 8
Catechism at the Doll Collector's House 10
Alfalfa Music 12
Dia de los Muertos 14
Sanitarium, Guadalajara 16
Pismo, 1959 18

II.

Brothers 23
"Bobbin Boy in a Mill in Chicopee, Mass., 1911,"
      A Photograph by Lewis W. Hine 26
Letter from a New Widow to Her Son/*after Williams* 28
Night-Song in Verano 31
Delta Landlady 33
Oil and Blue 35
Iron 37

III.

At the Rainbow 41
California Sonnets: Night Sequence 43
To a Pair of Lovers Cast in Plaster 47

Paper Diamond 49
For Frances 51
Willing Witnesses 53

IV.
The Least of Palms 59

Notes 65

PART ONE

Coyotes

I've bicycled out
into the blue fieldlight
to glimpse them: a few flecks
zigzagging down a hillside,
drawn to the locked compounds

igniting at this hour
and echoing the sky. Before long
they stop, shy of a smell
or barbed wire, circling
on old pissed-on ground

yellowed once more, and wait.
Once, as a child in a field
flush with poppies, I found
a carcass, split open
and shelled of all gray

sponge-like organs, the heart
and lungs gone from this vest
of coyote, the head
still intact, the jaws
squinched upward and open.

That night, in a dream
or awake, I heard the canine
dark flourish, unchecked
like wisteria, climbing
nightlong into my room. "Awful,"

one could say, like frayed notes
from the trumpet I would soon
give up, the brass valves—"Three
throats," my teacher once said—
suffering all that spit. "It's all

just vibrations in the air,"
Mr. Sessions would say, half
joking and half in awe when we
were all in tune. But out there
I imagined the splayed

pelt was shuddering, gathering
the field's orange swirl and sway
blowing into it, the troubled
snout fluent once more and firing
its off-key aria that singes

the dark. Now I lie
between thistle and buttercups,
belly down and thick
with childhood's prolonged pain,
and under the clear polish

of moonlight I watch three
long skulls tilt back
as if they could sing
down the moon: a remnant bone
summoned back and willing to rise.

Belief

for Jon and Ernesto

There are those—old aunts, far-off
godparents—whose houses seem ready
for ghosts: east of Madera, bricked
and scarred in the last century,
is the house my mother's aunt
lit candles in (though wired
for lights in '38; her parlor
nightly sent forth a dozen
"flamedrops"). A Stevens .22 pump
was found in the cellar, and a woman
in a black nightgown cried and walked
from shadows to the outhouse.
She was dead; she rose
some nights the way clouds
of insects lift from long grass—dark
breath of the earth, brief, wind-broken. . . .
Take care, they warn, these
death-long witnesses of grief
any hour can dole out, unresolved,
and flood the soul. Aunt Esther
gestured back with wick yarn alone.
"But don't worry," she said. "Most
never glimpse one; even more
think you're nuts if you do." But

belief can start anywhere, even here
in a plum orchard, wind-stirred
and radiating leaf-spurs, or out beyond
the old washroom where "someone
you can't touch, some stranger
doing eternal chores, touches you."

Early Morning Test Light
Over Nevada, 1955

Your mother slept through it all,
her face turned away
like the dark side of the earth.

We'd heard between *rancheras*
on the radio
that the ladles
and the two bears
that lie among the stars
above Nevada
would fade at 3:15 as though seared
by a false sun.

The stove exhaled all night
a trinity of blue rings. You entered
your fourth month
of floating in the tropical,
star-crossed water
your mother carried under her heart
that opens and closes
like a butterfly.

When the sky flared,
our room lit up. Cobwebs

sparkled on the walls, and a spider
absorbed the light
like a chameleon and began
to inch toward the outer rings
as if a fly trembled.

Roosters crowed. The dog
scratched at the door. I went outside
hearing the hens and thought *weasel*
and found broken eggs, the chicks
spongy, their eyes
stunned and shrouded
by thin veils of skin.

"Don't open your eyes,"
I whispered to you when darkness
returned. I thought of your bones
still a white gel, I remembered the story
of blood smeared on doorways,
and I placed my hand on the balloon
you rode in—that would slowly sink
to your birth. I said
the Old German name your mother already picked
for you, *Robert.* It means *bright fame.*

Catechism at the Doll Collector's House

for the "believer in total immersion"

We were herded, some dragged, down
Lotus Street to the house
of unblinking glass eyes, the glass
of insomnia. Dolls
ruled everywhere: on shelves,
underneath end tables, silent
committees packed in closets,
all as clean and cool-eyed
as the nuns who hushed our mouths.

"This one's my favorite,"
Mrs. Holly once said, and she pointed
to a Dutch farmgirl, her left eye
missing, her tight wooden shoes
filled with straw and glue.
And in the language of staring,
which the nuns mistook for prayer
and blessed me coming and going,
I confessed—why I can't recall—
to that one blue eye
that the first wafer
placed on my tongue I chewed
and spat out, that the figurine
of Mary, found broken and buried

under a sofa, lost her head
beneath the rocker's wood,
curved like a Persian sword,
that was swung by the weight
of my small buttocks,
and I did not confess.

So many witnesses
who couldn't scream.
Raggedy Ann's mouth was black thread
zigzagged and perfect.
The Foreign Legionnaire stared out
over the sand in the fishbowl
and tried to forget. Even
the ballerina, lifted up in the bathroom,
suffered my clumsy aim:
urine missed the bowl and spotted
her white lace, a clown in polka dots
her sad partner. I sprinkled
Lily Dust to hide the stains,
the odor of powder already laced
throughout the rooms, the only evidence
in the house that someone else
could sweat and smell like me.

Alfalfa Music

for you on Poppy Street

Erik the Swede knew how to treat
those bulls. They had their own
minnowed water troughs—their pens
filled with their own beloved smack.
All day they stood and stared, complete
with squalling halos of flies, alone
with their milk-faith in glands,
each one mapped in white and black.

Cousins steamed up the stalls
long before stainless hookups
became the ganglia of the place.
Those well-bred teats would swell
like huge counterweights; all
that liquid worry built up
via hay and four stomachs: grace
of a kind, the farm kind, that welled

within the great-veined bags.
They were fat girls and stank, sired
by those three ear-tagged dolts.
The Cityedge Holstein Farm
at milking time was all iron
in the air—neck-bell notes;

alfalfa music, it still lags
somewhere, wall-eyed and warm.

Dia de los Muertos

for Lowry

November, zinnias late
and lifting toward nightshade.
A boy I know plays dead,
unaware of the blood-orange
nimbuses that sweep by, heaven
withheld from a face
partial to rain and squalls
of color at sunset. When porchlights
turn mothy, his father
will whistle him in, this kid
who can shake off death
like so much grit and grass
at evening's end. Houselights
will blink off, and mothers
will take fathers to bed,
and a child nuzzling sleep
will hear cries
which might be the groans
of the dying or the groans
of love. . . .

And I'm the neighbor
gone loveless for years
and walled off by eucalyptus

and brick. I'm the silent one
drawn to bonfires, those
in alleyways and in the sky,
who finger-traces the flamelights
that blue and smoke out, leaf
upon leaf, star upon star.
I must become flame-like to go
beyond bucktoothed fences
and horse stalls and a horse's neigh;
I must inchworm my way
up a cindery path, believing
the Dog Star will yield
its back and ferry me across
the blue-black fathoms.
I'd like to think
that heaven's long acres
are scored with roses, island roses
belled open by the bees
with their true appetite
for all orders that bloom.

Sanitarium, Guadalajara

1. The Letter

At last we see her
among all the women half-shadowed
and waiting: our aunt
holding an ashtray, her hair clipped
like a boy's, her thin face
barely recognized. Her last letter,
the first written with her left hand,
bore the scrawl of a child and said,
"Part of me has died. Now the other half
lives alone and remembers."

She wrote of crows that swooped down
and pecked her head in a bean field
in '38, on the Day of the Dead, and they spoke
". . . in tongues unlike priests, unlike
any holy sound all women near death
bow to. They were *brujos*,"
and she called out their names
to her stunned sisters and neighbors.
"And I began to kiss the earth and thought
of the soiled feet of Jesus."

2. The Songbook

"This is my room, my small country.
And that the window where my face
stares and smiles at the moon
behind the asylum of clouds.
I smile because the trees nearby
hold the small bird that returned
after decades of darkness. He sings
above the crickets and whistles
the humanlike tunes that drifted
through the white gauze curtains
to a young girl years ago. . . .

"They are the songs, deep
in feathers, that must come out
and be sung from branch to bedside
to one with ears birdlike.
It is the songbook of empty boughs,
the music of moon phases, given
to those who lie awake, who listen
to the strains of creatures in trees,
breathing in trunk hollows, who know
the only songs worth singing
and passing on."

Pismo, 1959

The day ends with the blur
you wanted, full of watery hours,
the light weathered like aluminum,
gulls twining the air—summer's
floating script in the sky
refusing to pull together. The sun

breaks down each body
to silver, each bar of flesh
waist-deep in foam and brine.
The day flares out: wreckage
of orange on blue. Sea stars
wheel into place; like you,

they witness the tide, the whitecaps
tipped with distance, the distance
large with blown sails and spray.
And the whole beachway goes cold
while strands of ocean light
sink like heavy netting.

So this is the sun's passage
through dark doors of water. . . .
So this is the scrolled shell

on fire, magnified. There is no one—
no lifeguard—to call out all
the bathers from calling water,

though you sense the dark
roll in, grain by toe-felt grain,
its curl slick and seamless
like a wing or a wave. Home's
still a hundred miles inland. You say
the globe is three-fifths blue

and rocks forever toward us, you say
we will never die, and I believe.
I'll sleep the whole drive back
beside you, leaning close and small
like a shadow reeled in, your face
precise with fine sand and shining.

PART
TWO

Brothers

for Joey

Your fist twitching late in the night
and I would like to say *Easy now*
to calm your fingers
thick as carrots we once pulled
from the earth   But I don't
for years we haven't touched palms
caked with soil
or bled together on the same rosebush
our hands cut and held out
to our limping mother

That was years ago   Now
I come into the house
alone   everyone asleep   and place
my pants and cologne-scented shirt
next to yours
stiff from the day's cement
our father passed on to you
as though on a trowel and said
Take it

Outside   a star plops
into the pool   Or is it
an apricot from the neighbor's tree

Or the body of an angel
one of those we thought   as children
fell throughout the night and bore
the sad face of Jesus
carved by fire and darkness
Or is it the face I see   lit
by the cold light
of the moon   in the mirror
my eyes blurred and half lit
like the profiled moon   my lips
saying silently
Who are you hitting   and one ear
turned to you in darkness

The cold street air pops
as a motorcycle carries off
into the night the scream
of every man who loses
his brother   the rider losing himself
in the tailpipe's throat
in the mixture of gas
and air   in the fumes
taking on the gray shape of a man
no one holds

Soon   when my dream begins
I will whisper to you
about the cement that hardens
my groin   about the rosebush petals
tinted with our blood
I will turn my face
to one side   like the moon
and expose it to the harsh streetlamp
in your dream   and let you
hit the face of night and air
I've come to be

"Bobbin Boy in a Mill in Chicopee, Mass., 1911," A Photograph by Lewis W. Hine

for Ken Butler

Someone will see you, standing
in a mill in Chicopee, Massachusetts,
and think the single thought
that runs along the greased mind
of America: work. But there was more.
You left work at night and returned
ten hours later, still night,
to the mill's humming note.
The sunlight of your childhood
came between the heavy bars
that crisscrossed the brick windows.
You became a bobbin boy and worked
like a man, a boy who entered
dark corridors and came out a man
who changed the spinning spools
of yarn that kept the hands
of Minnesota warm, a boy
who looked up after work
and saw the stars loom and weave
the patterns of the coming years.
You dreamt of walking the bright
corridors of a school, loving
the small voices out of rhythm,
and the threads that dangled from coats

were short or cut off and couldn't run
into the next decade. But you
woke up and left for the building
shaped like a church, and once inside,
where the pews should be, you knelt
between the mechanically-long rows
and heard, in Chicopee, Massachusetts,
in the dark mill, cold and heavy,
the one hymn being sung to the foreman,
high in his cage where the pulpit
should be, who looked down
on it all and, years later, like
everyone else, would claim innocence.

Letter from a New Widow
to Her Son/*after Williams*

for Geronimo Vasquez, 1892–1983,
and his wife, Petra, and their son, Jose

It was as though the night tides
he swam in years ago as a child
overtook him at last, and left him
calm as a starfish. Sixty-nine years
we slept together in these hills
still tracked with our footprints
that linger on without us
beneath the wind-swelled trees.
Now his face, scrubbed gray
as the moon, arcs across the windows
of my dreams, his forehead
fringed with moss, his eyes
struck with the light of all
his bruised phases. Last night
I dreamt he hovered over a little boy
and dared to kiss him only while he slept;
it turns out all this happened
fifty-five years ago
above your own sleep-saddened face.

Soon, you say, you'll come back,
and too late as well. Today
I stared at the giant lily pads,
newly risen in the warm water

he taught you to swim in, that now haunt
the pond's sky that seems so shrunken
like your childhood. He's out there
under the grassy rise, not far
from where the first house donkey lies,
the one you once rode
while he trotted, blindfolded, in a circle
and drove the millstone,
long since cracked apart, that now anchors
his name to the earth. One night
he came back, old dead Luis, to your father,
as though the bullet never entered
his long-eared brain, and your father swore
he saw Luis stamp and turn
in a blue hoop of light
as though harnessed to the moon itself.
Silly man, I thought. Now they lie
beyond the sea-tugging moon.

Sixty-nine years. Mornings
I rise to open the windows
for two wild parakeets who nest
high in the kitchen rafters,
and I still crack eggs

for two, and brush away a stray feather
that greens his empty chair. I imagine you
outside in your far November
burning leaves, standing close to the fire
you tend and prod upward with a stick,
watching the ashes, the black alphabet
of elm and apricot trees, staining the air
like a child's scrawl. And like a child
you'll look up at the clouds,
their huge faces chiseled
by the wind. Like you, the clouds
are headed for nightfall, shedding
small tufts like clipped hair, punctured
by the horns of geese, *nimbuses,*
your father once told you, filled
with the moist, brooding memory
of their maker, the ocean.

Night-Song in Verano

for Peter and the twin

A strange song blooms
in the dark. It's my neighbor,
born in toolshed
during the war, and she sings
a song the widows of Italy sang
to old men and the children
of dead fathers. She and her mother
sailed out third class in '48 and waved
to no one on the soldierless docks.
Her mother let go of her
years ago, and waits
six miles north
under fine Carrara marble
that followed the same ocean route.

And now the long vowels
call out to the fields
of childhood. An old song
reappears, hidden cargo
ferried between the continents
of the dead and the living,
and rises above the whirr
of laundry and crickets. A song
clear as the cold-blue moon

ladders up and lingers,
a high note slow
as the sky's stone, song
and stone burning with the echo
of light so far-off—
the throat yielding and the woman too,
having crossed the black Atlantic
and no longer pressed for time.

Delta Landlady

What I wake up to? The slow cargo
of nimbuses; valley and river
fog; yesterday's rainbow, its arc-freight
rain-clean and calm—the sky's asylum.
But today it's winter bulbs, off-white
"hearts" she calls them, my old landlady,

Danish—a good heart, as landladies
go. All day she trowels for spring's cargo:
turbaned tulips; "they're kin to the white
lily family," and line rivers
she knew in pre-war, pre-asylum-
in-the-States days. She derailed freight

trains; planted explosives and saw freight
cars "spill like toys" (so my landlady
claims). One night she pulled out asylum
papers stamped in New York. "The cargo
ship *Jutland* docked in the East River:
my point of entry." From there to White

Plains; her first stateside lot was all white
sand and concrete, two blocks from the freight
yards. Soon other towns, other rivers

with their residues. My landlady's
album's thick with her man, doomed cars. "Go
back too much and you'll want asylum

from those days, or today. Asylum's
the last thing," she said. Now her small white
dogs keep close watch as nearby cars go
zooming by, solid with cold sun-freight
and flash. There's a club, *Birdland* (ladies
night's on Wednesdays), that's a jammed river

of delta tourists on Blue River
Street; the house band's name is Asylum
Door. But guess what?—my old landlady
told *me* of the place. She met Nash White
there: a longshoreman, long-armed from freight
work, who unknotted rain-flecked cargo

sea rivers yield, the banks black and white
with dogs; egret asylums; freighters;
this landlady and the heart's cargo.

Oil and Blue

for Wenders and Raye Leen

She might be a straggler
from the late show,
bothered by French lives
subtitled as sad as hers;
she might sense how the dark
veins of the Pacific
push up toward the luminous
spokes of the Fun Zone; she may. . . .
But what do I know of strangers
strange with God knows what—
is it *longing?*

       I loiter and stare
for me and for her: a woman
harborside and alone,
walking the rim
of boat stalls. She yields
here and there to long
scarves of light
the fouled bay repeats,
electric yellows and reds
blown down from mastlines—
party lights riveting

a cross in the May tide.
They flash like fish. . . .

       No matter;
I'll never know her,
though we both stare hard
at all the briny lamps
flaring up in a corridor
of water: filaments
a body would burn
if it could, the scorched traces
just beyond her hand
descending to palm
intangible colors
warped in oil and blue.

Iron

Corroding elbows, U-joints, and Briggs
couplings kick at the cold.
All night you must tolerate
pipes that moan and knock,

these noisy neighbors just beyond
wallpaper geese. Outside, the rooms
in the orchards frost over,
and the moon's long claw

cleaves November. It was here
my parents once bandaged their lives,
their faces troubled beneath strips
of gauzy moonlight, the room's

gathered pain pure as Madera ice.
Now they are gone, asleep
twenty miles from this house
where webs cup the high corners,

where a man can curl in bed
and reinvent the embryonic winter
he set out from. And far from traffic
spinning away in its own wind

and anger, these caves of breath
taste good on nights like this, the pipes
releasing into the numb world
all that should ache even through iron.

PART THREE

At the Rainbow

for Linda, Theresa, and Phyllis

At fifteen, shaving by then, I passed
for eighteen and got in, in where alcoves
breathed with ill-matched lovers—
my sisters among them—who massed
and spun out their jagged, other selves.
I saw the rhythmic dark, year over

year, discharge their flare: they scored
my memory, adrift now in the drifting place.
Often I watched a slow song empty
the tabled sidelines; even the old poured
out, some dragged by wives, and traced
odd box shapes their feet repeated. *Plenty*

and *poor:* thoughts that rose as the crowd
rose—my sisters too—in the smoked air.
They rise on. . . . They say saxophones
still start up Friday nights, the loud,
troubled notes wafting out from where
I learned to lean close and groaned

into girls I chose—no, took—and meant it.
In the Rainbow Ballroom in Fresno
I sulked, held hands, and wheeled among

the deep-bodied ones who reinvented
steps and turns turned fast or slow,
and this body sang, man to woman, song to song.

California Sonnets: Night Sequence

for the baby doctor

1.

I look up at the night's broad back
gone crazy with tattoos of light, seasonal
signs almost beyond stoppage, and let
the unsayable build skyward. As it is
I've put off sleep, its gray tunnel
circular and face-filled, to take in
pulse-points that work the peninsular dark.
Last night, below the ridge that blocks
out the ocean's amplitude, a woman
called me to bed. And slow's the sprawl
of the almost-in-love, their wave and blur
charging their own amplitude. Yielding, we took
to the windowsill, like children almost, the curtains
blown wide as if calling the star-sprawl in, almost.

2.

Witness the Bear's stoked belly, his burning
stupor commanding the rooftops. . . . Of course
this changes nothing: by morning the windows
are wing-sliced; all day the languid ladies
of the field and wild cowpeas still carry
hillsides into spring; the oak's true
posture of pain deepens. But I know,
due to celestial warp, some stars are black
cinders where they seem to blaze: scars
of light that survive the body. Dead suns
do that; they haunt with their ghost-lit patinas;
they reach us with their fixed and mapped
movements, like old lovers: pliable arcs of light,
they come on inarticulate, glassy, and sure.

3.

For the nightsky's vault issues insomnia,
someone said, those troubled hours withholding
the passage and balance good sleep drifts back to.
In Los Altos I join the bare-knuckled ones
who browse the neoprene bags and dumpster spillage.
And my nose swells with the road-smear of skunk, not
the living kind that will not scare, but a tire-
smashed stripe, creamy clear, almost afloat.
They say eternity's a channel in the sky.
—As if the skunk soul veers upward and drafts
like a kite.—As if the skunk angels
could spot this small jaywalker, stalled
like the number 1, beneath the intersections
of heaven. —As if I were in love.

4.

Out of the fissured dark, columbine will mount,
suffer, and sustain acres of thistle and mud;
the high, plain shouts of children
half-heard a block away at recess will strive
to twine the day together. Bells and mission. But
before you rise from sleep's wash, think of raccoons
arrogant on Dixon Way, who palm chicken bones
before they rehouse the flood drains; think
of me hogging a whole street the way ladles
hog zones in the sky. Think how the wintered
and rolling earth reveals itself, how
everything the night holds out and clarifies,
like love, withdraws suddenly from the limbs
and organs of intake: hands, eyes, and heart.

To a Pair of Lovers Cast in Plaster

for George Segal

I knew a woman blue
as Segal's *Blue Girl*
on a Black Bed: her lover
a long bruise, asleep,
and no one save the sculptor
to witness her bedside stare
at nothing.

       For in that queer
light after lovemaking, she too
would sit and eye her arms
as though waiting for sores
welling up like fog.
She wouldn't notice the moon
and May wind shutting down
branch by branch, the leaves
stilled high in the elms as if
a room gone silent and gray
walled them in as well.

       Her face,
if seen at such times,
would go unrecognized
by those whose love was more

than piecemeal: the crewcut son
in basic training, the daughter
sworn off of sugar and red meat.
But Segal would know her;
he'd dab on the plaster
until it scabbed her whole body
and lover as well, adding
those two related hues
borne by the collapsing mattress
and flesh beyond all repair.

Paper Diamond

The hour's all April wind and sunset.
From your high bedroom windows
we watch his kite spool out
and waver and strain—as we did

moments ago, the blue percale
lightly soured from our lovemaking.
And you're troubled, not by the dragon
addicted to wind and tethered

to patient ten-year-old hands,
but by yourself: a woman whose son
can take a hint and go test
the blown acres of sky above alfalfa.

And what of me, whose desire
barely tugged can crazily climb,
who can witness this pain
even while loving? Tell me of a kite

that doesn't signal longing or loss,
whose paper diamond doesn't bless the sky
and link sad earth to heaven,
mother to son, or you to me. . . .

Something the wind can take—
thin wooden cross, tail of linen,
twine—waits to be reeled in,
snapped, or simply released.

For Frances

A faint sea wind, long-traveled
like a wish, finds the doors
of your eyes opened to Orion
and connecting the luminous dots.

I want to believe you yield at last
to a starward tide, the neighborhood
gone silent, the sky's barge
endless with its burning cargo.

And why not now, drained
as you are—no music, no love
bandaged with kisses—and lost
under moons of grape and berry?

Father dozes on the porch, his lap
dark with his arthritic terrier—July's
old sleepers called away
from the ghost-wash of fireflies

rising, claiming the eggplants
webbed with silver like your hair.
What finally summons you back
flourishes behind your watered roses:

children gather for *Hide and Seek*
among thorny shadows, their playful
passage briefly lit by cries
as indecipherable as you are to me.

Willing Witnesses

for Jean and Dixie

1.

For months you've been here, hidden
by fallen dogwood, with termites winged
and blossoming in the air. What's left of you
shines beneath tangles of March light:
your rib cage a trellis for wildflowers
creeping toward heaven, your hind leg
cracked by the trap
once set yawning by the river your tongue loved.
The moon's curved flame
lit the lamp of the river and you came,
prodded by the wick of pure thirst.

Someone has clipped your skull off your body
like a rose, leaving you
to take on the color of starlight,
to fill with poppies called up by your ruin.
Someone left you to be named and furred
by imagination. Someone knelt over and released you
from the long, steel kiss of your going.

2.

Once, high in a tree, going
for the last winter oranges, I found
three dead hatchlings—*robins* I thought.
Their bowl of twigs held cotton
from junked sofas, the foil
of *Juicyfruit,* and a red rubberband.
The birds were hard, their wings like old rubber,
their beaks still open.
Had I found them still in their blue shells
like Easter candies, I would have watched them,
one by one, hit the cement below
like heavy balls of spit.
I was nine years old.

3.

Somewhere, Penny, along this slab of river
where everything greens, you are long dead.
We named you after the copper hue
your eyes hoarded, like the pennies
in tiny trouser pockets I jingled to call you.

But your eyes tarnished as you went blind,
and you shook like a child
locked in a dark room. It was a Sunday.
We waited in the car, by the bridge
that has since crumbled like you, and cursed
our father who hit you with a brick
and tossed your brown seven pounds
into the willows that hugged the bank.

I was long in coming back,
ignoring the Sunday light that called and called,
echoing over the years of tall grass,
this light that flowers along the river
brooding in a cold bed of stones,
the river and the light your only willing witnesses
who know where you rest,
waiting for the rustle of coins.

PART
FOUR

The Least of Palms

Had Williams practiced in
failing Madera, calling
on Mrs. Thomas, still sore
and breast-feeding *the gift*

*from that long-gone
motherfucker,* he'd notice
Poppy's cinder lots blooming
with ripped sofas, the brick

light of ash and fine
ash grit in the air—irritants
the Doc's own eyewash
couldn't fully wash out.

For one deep grain is
all it takes to aggravate
an eye focused on the local
throb of things: soured

canalway that oozed
the nine months' wonder; curdy
scum-mass of newsprint
brooding in gutterponds

where sun-fragments
dance. Some baby's loud all
could be the day's first
scribbled note, then roses

and barrel-staves—whatever
his black bag would swing by
and those hands that would open
and reach into its aah.

*   *   *

This door-to-door salesman
had no nose; rather, a quarter-
sized hole drew his skin
in. He seemed forever

snorting in the noon porchlight,
clearing the sinus canals,
the phlegm that would not
ease, even in sleep.

With a polio leg
she lifted for years—years

of my not noticing—
   and still lifts, my mother

always opened the door
for his pitch: *Last chance. . .*
NO PEDDLARS went ignored
   and neighbors bought

   what they could. When fog
bloomed, doors soaked up the gray
   and went unknocked. Bells
    unrung. They said *His hole*

   clogs seasonal—breathes
through his mouth all November.
   They found him in bed, his walls
    loaded with snapshots: our doors,

   our palms blurring back.
We own them still, knuckle and fog,
   brush or bowl: unwanted goods
    always invited in.

   *   *   *

It's all nuance. I remember
fucking this woman who loved
    to watch my cock
    take her wrinkles out

    down there; laughing,
she'd flex and guffaw
    so hard she didn't care
    if the rubber broke,

    "It's all *dick*-tion,"
she'd say, forgetting to feed
    the *Magic Fingers* bed
    its quarters—hell,

    we even forgot the clock.
There'd be that faint
    ring of blood
    just below the glans

    where the foreskin broke—
not enough *K-Y* and far
    too horny back then—
    and stung afterwards

while she washed me down.
And I soaped her. We talked
about childhood baths
of all things, the *Lava* bar

passed and palmed as we
remembered selves in other tubs,
other erased lives that once
could rise whole.

*   *   *

The sun's low disc
seems to skid or drag—
if you wished, it could plow
everything under. Some days

I bicycle until I'm lost,
not knowing why, and somehow
pedal my way back, one
elm-shadowed block

at a time—piecemeal
passage and blur, the way

all years cog and click,
　　blessed or shot: it's

　'63, November's
TV funeral a week old, the tube-
　snow the first sign: nothing
　　stays clear. Who'd guess

　three years later I'd see
Bobby at Roeding Park
　stumping for Pat Brown
　　one August night. My father

　suffered me shoulder-high
so I could see. . . . As for the words:
　upswept with my balloon,
　　beyond recall. And downwind

　the sky's flotilla grew
and shrank as wish-filled hands
　opened and emptied, some as small
　　as mine—the least of palms.

Notes

"Catechism at the Doll Collector's House": The dedication's quotation is from Elizabeth Bishop's poem "At the Fishhouses."

"Dia de los Muertos": The title means Day of the Dead; the italicized lines are from Malcolm Lowry's novel *Under the Volcano.*

The various forms— "steps and turns turned fast or slow"—are intentional.

You say we'll never die, today.